BEFORE THE DROUGHT

Margo Berdeshevsky

Glass Lyre Press

Copyright © 2017 Margo Berdeshevsky
Paperback ISBN: 978-1-941783-39-9

All rights reserved: except for the purpose of quoting brief passages for review, no part of this book may be reproduced or transmitted in any form or by any means, electronic or mechanical, including photocopying, recording, or by any information storage and retrieval system, without permission in writing from the publisher.

Cover art: © Margo Berdeshevsky
Author photo: Tina Garzero
Design & layout: Steven Asmussen
Copyediting: Linda E. Kim

Glass Lyre Press, LLC
P.O. Box 2693
Glenview, IL 60025
www.GlassLyrePress.com

. . . and a word / of rescue from the great eyes —Muriel Rukeyser

Praise for *Before the Drought*

("Drought" (Middle English, from Old English *drūgath*, from *drūgian*) dates back to the twelfth century, and, as with many of our earliest words, articulates a primal human condition—in this case thirst, want, dearth. With the temporal, shape-shifting fluidity of myth, *Before the Drought* is both lambent with pre-Lapsarian plenitude and vexed by post-Lapsarian lack. The speaker in these poems—part transgressive nun, part revolutionary alchemist—confronts at every turn what it means to live in time, in a body ("how unexpectedly you age / . . . . My strutter, my ogre, my mirror-bitch brayer"), and nonetheless steadfastly to hold an abiding trust in the slaking, annealing replenishment of the broken-open anything—heart, body, sky, heavens.

—Lisa Russ Spaar

Margo Berdeshevsky's *Before The Drought* issues from hermetically concealed ether, evolving into view as elliptically kindled ballet, as beatific trance. The poems exist as prescient pre-destined sermons speaking inside themselves via inter-active marrow, via en-livened speculation. All the while they sustain themselves by means of arcane classical moisture etched with hints of erotic juniper not unlike the textured "skin" of ashen "silk." Thus, the writing in this collection spontaneously forms into a verbal tapestry of incremental brilliance.

—Will Alexander

Contents

—1—

Blason Pour le Corps	11
Whisper	12
Cut	14
Whose Sky, Between	16
Here is My Body	18
Pulse	19
What Was I Waiting For?	20
No Modifier At All	21
Listening to Sky	22

—2—

Before the Drought	27

—3—

Paris, Chérie	33
On Evenings of Exceptional Calm	35
Stilled Summer	37
A Place It Might Be All Right To Die	39
Before Noon	41
Yes, the Lights	42
Stopped for Hours—	44

—3 (con't)—

12—2014	46
After Fado, at the Elgins	48
Beyond My Used-up Words…	50

—4—

Born By Knife	55
Shears	56
Half Moon Holy	58
My Friends Speak	59
One Blessing	60
Native	61
Almost Untitled/ But Never Without Flames:	62
Adaptation	63

—5—

For Sisters Everywhere, Even On St Valentine's Day	67
In Passage / Passage / Passage	68
But Of The River Too	69
Only Looking For Her Double Headed Tribe,	70
Blason	71
Straw Bird Of Shadow, Be An Owl	73
It Was The Door Of Faith, And	75
A Promise	77

Before My Death	81
Stage Fright	82
Evil Twin Of Blue	83
In Custody of the Eyes	84
Mornings After—	86
Raising Her Eyelids	88
One—Will Not Fall	89
Dusk	90
Notes	95
Acknowledgments	97
About the Author	99

— I —

Blason Pour le Corps

Gentle, the sound of the rain —Verlaine

Clitoris, belly,
nape, taste bud,
body-beloved-bully,
how surprisingly you strut,
how unexpectedly you age—
How night rides the in and the out of you
Seine of you—doe of you
Who raped the silk in you? (Don't answer,)
blood's hummingbird
under your ribs
Body-monster, ravenous
now the hound's heartbeat
outrunning my greed
Body, inside,
thin ibis, flaming—
mirror-bitch brayer do I love you, or not?
Body my blessing   my birth day bleed.
Body my deceiver
Body my taunt
My strutter, my ogre, my mirror-bitch brayer
We're as opened as we'll ever be.
Listen. Listen.
Verlaine's—new rain.

~

Whisper

Why does my skin want me in her
does she know she's holding a woman in?

Not burning does she ache when the wildfires shout
Does she know how many Septembers she's given

Am I nailed inside her, cell by cell
pale veil sewn womb to sky

— is she mine or am I her
pet cobra whispering like rocks

in the streambed for more passion more
tenderness more friction more killing —

Do the stones and the branches want out?
Does my skin want tattoos of hard young men

or skulls or sentences or swallow-corpses
fallen— If I give her all my wars, my only

eye— will she let me sleep will she hold my
night dirges until I can remember them

When I die, skin of silk, skin of ash, skin
of my century, will she forgive me

again when the leaves are all dropped
Why have a woman in you — skin

Why not a bone mountain
Why not a better prayer than this one

If you won't answer, skin of my skin
skin of my woman-ing —

There are knives that might.

~

Cut

Soleil cou coupé —Apollinaire

While they whispered of frayed days like knots
on an old nun's robe-tie, her nakedness hidden
under dark cloth

While they lunched on garlic snails blessed
one afternoon by the Seine — one
with a lover's arms to bed in that night, one
with none, *but Paris...*

While they whispered sham & disaster of
presidents, the bomb that almost but
didn't kill last night, the darker-eyed of the two
begged the other *read Levi's "The Drowned*

and the Saved" — while each knew it
was such a Monday, such a September to
choose or not to if not this afternoon
next week

While the lighter-eyed one swerved a bee from
her face and the other swatted it from hers until
each cringed to not be stung, one
lifted her empty wine glass knowing how to

capture a bee in flight & stifle, trapped it
between tablecloth & overturned bell jar, it
bleated they didn't hear its cry inside, it kicked
thin legs & turned over & turned over its

gold body while they whispered of ends
of time & one of them kept looking at it dying
not stinging them & when she couldn't watch
the dying any longer, slid the glass & its capture

toward the table's edge act of mercy act of shame
& the glass tipped, fell, the bee fell out the slipped
glass shattered & the waiter watched
& he applauded —

~

Whose Sky, Between

A name that meant sound of an owl's hard fall, another day of blood gunned to all
walls, a tiredness of how well we mourn. How well I do not pray. How well we tried.

When at night I go to sleep/ fourteen angels watch do keep... strewing me with
roses ... as my soul reposes ...God will not forsake me ... when dawn at last will wake me ...

Love from among almond trees, a girl says, girl in a killer country where sun spills
floral bloods. I've plucked one almond from a branch, she says, her borders killed

by the same or other arms that kill us here. A symphony of cicadas, frogs or other
friends, she adds, counting minutes on her fingers. Girl who asked me once if her God

would kill her if she loved orgasm, unfastened her veil, exposed her thighs to a star.
I send her burned love from an island, whispers through veils of ironwood needles, their

spill on a shore I share with a darker sun, with a man weary of quest or prayer.
Our hands take no longer to renew than light of a silvered solstice.

No longer to hold than cumulous too high to reach, too near to misunderstand.
Dragon-eyes and fat-thighed cloud-leaps chase old friendship as we do, hold

afternoon as we hold light's fall across no-color winds. No colored prayers.
Yes, my ocean is dying, my friend says. Yes, I know, I have said. My culture is dead,

he says. Yes, I bend, asking because he whispered among other trees, once, on an
island, once: *live in the question*. And there, I know I believed.

Of the elements that are poisoned, now — earth, yes, waters, yes, the air, — we mouth —
is fire the one that will live? Ask, rocked by a day's burnt hands here, kneel while the war-bent

are kissed by the drowned in another sea. Let's not mourn. Imagine almonds. A symphony
of cicadas born to live for a day. In the long clouds, our own most recent dead live in the after,

know the zero point landings of owls. Here, dragons, between hidden gods.
How many? How hot is fire, is it a desire to age, or to forget? Grace, to the wind.

I pray less, my friend says. Yes, but will fire be what stays?
Ask the ironwoods that once, I heard, were cut and nailed to form the Cross,

if this is love—
and whose sky, between?

This day, how many white cranes remember all the bombs we've made to make the 'other'
dead. Said: so we may never die. Said: hang a thousand small wings from our branches.

May one crane fly, one jasmine open, one thrush sing — all fragile night. One bloom of
a peace that cannot die.

. . . Because we will remember: blooms of jellyfish, men-o-war, and men of war,
long ravenous ancient fossils said to overtake all seas of life. They never die. They clone.

~

Here is My Body

Invisible, on our lake, our dreamscape, the old blue heron lands. Beak of my hunger. Beak of her hunger. Beak of her mothering. Mother-me, I say. I'm her body of surrender, waiting. I'm her body of hunger, waiting. Her body of danger, waiting under the five million star-fall night. Mother, I cry, you promised kinder dreams. You promised sleep. Be kind, you said, before you surrendered. Before you climbed the star-fall. This night won't last, you said. I'm the heron, I'm the lake at peace, our vine leads to you, you said. Your body of surrender, waiting, I whisper . . . the blue heron will feed us. Blue dawn will delete us. Peace. Our bodies will sleep. Our danger will sleep. I will love you, you said. That was my promise, before. Our lake waits. Don't cry, I said. Here is my body, I said. Sleep. The hungry beaks will feed. Even sparrows…winged ones…our old promise is kept, this night. This dangerous, last, mothering-us night.

PULSE

Showers of snow geese.

Mirrors weren't my friends anymore, couldn't stand what they showed me, the changing flesh, thinning hair that used to reach my knees, the drowning of names in a mud-thick water mind

the shorter breaths. But the voice of my ghost was kind. He told me it would end, soon. Touch me,
I begged. He didn't but the geese began to rain every day, and I hummed for the blind to come near.

Showers of snow geese. The morning sky bled them, no one else noticed or was bothered. I covered my eyes the way I always had when I passed any accident in the street, so afraid to see

anything dead. Afraid of winter branches, rotting gardens, abandoned houses. I hummed, like the purr of a crone panther on her rock on a dry mountain. Hummed, so the blind came nearer.

You want so badly to be seen you'd paint eyes on the lids of the blind, my ghost said. A baritone, sung between the notes of tumbling snow geese. He was my ghost, I heard him, I did what I was

told. Always so afraid to be near in any way—to what didn't breathe. I wanted and needed to be seen
alive. Praised for being. For breathing, for not killing any enemies, for being a good girl, for being

a good woman, for becoming a knowing crone. You want so badly to be seen you would paint eyes on the lids of the blind, the ghost had said. *Yes*, I mouthed. *True*.

My enemy had had a bad accident. The car had exploded on a curve and I crawled away. Soon, the geese. Soon, my ghost. Soon, the rock on a slope of a sun-warm mountain and my own low

voice calling for the blind all night, until I was found holding a small white dog, my trembling fingers stroking and stroking the lids of her chilled milk soft eyes.

I wanted to forgive something. Someone. I stroked the dog. I stroked my heart, until blindly it broke all the way open, and one bird fell out. It was not blind. It was dead. But it hummed.

~

What Was I Waiting For?

After seeing the caves, Picasso said of modern art, "We have discovered nothing"

The new animal voice cries for my empty bed
Silk-tongued as cave paintings spread in menstrual reds.

All our wars in the tongues of the night-scarved
crows. Our mothers admit— and pretend to forget—

A wide red wing, climbing my cotton gown.
One sky's thickened milk, to feed arias, in silence.

Bed of old bloods asleep through dreams, and revenants
Un-paint my own riddles— open— here are my hands—

Would I mix my lost poems to a color not spoken in wars—
Did our mothers' souls die— while we waited?

Wild horsemen, sketched beast-men, were you drawn
in fact by girls afraid to tell secrets to their mothers?

~

No Modifier At All

None. No one is not connected to someone else in the city who was hurt that night or dead. It is the no-degrees of separation or escape. Or times we've been borne to. Everyone knows someone

who knew at least one in a city of millions. Open terraces under streetlamps and a fingernail of moon. Tables of friends. A concert by The Eagles of Death Metal and autumn and blood and no

breath and the young. The rifles and a will to end something. Paris, for lovers . . . I open my door to a man I've been calling all this week—to fix my door. Hamid, thin as a pencil, flaming as a showgirl.

A face from the projects. A face from the once-upon-colonies. My lock no longer works. These are days when one thinks of closing doors. He stands in my hall, eyes like tunnels and sewers that bend

under the city. Last Saturday there was a carnival bulging in those tunnels. People vowed to dance and to wear costumes and to live unless they die. I wore silk. Rented gowns, and feathers, and masks.

You had to be invited. Steps, underneath our city. I wore red. *Who are you,* someone whispered in the dark. *I don't know,* is anyone's reply. . . *I'm so sorry I have not answered you earlier in the week, Madame.*

My sister. The baby one. She is —, was one of—in the café. She came to the birthday for her lover. Her name was Djamila. I had photographed candles and flowers left for the murdered in front of that café, the day

after. I remember that name. *Djamila,* I tell him. His eyes are sewers, tunnels. He cries. I cry. *Destiny,* he mumbles so softly I am not sure I have heard. He pulls his satchel of tools into my hall to repair

my door. There is a noise somewhere, that is too loud. We are strangers. He has come to fix my door. Holding one another, until it is over. No modifier, at all.

~

for the Paris massacres in November 2015

Listening to Sky

And the true/ Joy of the long dead child sang burning/ In the sun. —Dylan Thomas

How a wandering albatross
can spend lives at sea
never returning to land.

With an act of humbled will—witnessing sky
a girl lifts and holds one thrumming gray
as mist or dying bird against her ear

a dial to know if it tells minutes
a beak to know if it might sound
the avian heartbeat to her brain-beat

the small folded body filled now with
that fog she stands alert in —listening—
fallen pearls, tell me of flight I'll

never be tell me of breath hidden
behind air too heavy with world.
There was a time, child of mornings

when she held a washed white sound
in the throat of its dove and sun
hovered with wider wings

and sun burned them
both. There was a time when
the silhouette of a raven stilled in flight

its skeleton ragged as omen
hovered in its place. There have been
times, for child and woman and those

who hear the sky. There have been mornings.
There has been joy. And there has not.
And I thought again of the albatross.

~

—2—

Before the Drought

The queen never asks why a crazy girl at her May Day table dances like each man's wet dream but is never satisfied, and the men never touch her. There is so much to do the girl says and says—kissing the cheeks of each of her neighbors who never touch her—so much to do she can't decide what, but she has to do it all, in case she dies. She doesn't kiss the queen who cannot cry. The queen can't cry. All she can do is hiss like the wind. And now, she doesn't know her subjects' names. Maybe she used to, but not now.

~

Against the far stone wall of her throne room a brazier pit has been lit, a huge pot is suspended, cooking the traditional soup all night. May Day for her guests, a table laid with sausages and cheeses and deep bowls and breads, roses at the door, so open they are distractingly flagrante. May Day, and the queen can't cry. She's tried again all night. She has provided musicians who play old songs until their fingers hurt and their strings break. There is a man at her table who has a silent wife, mother of a daughter whose name she now can no longer remember, or her own. Because she fell last week, because the blood hardened in the wrong way inside her head, because the nightingale forgot its aria that night and darkness was colored iodine instead, because orange spiders came instead of stars.

~

And the queen can't cry. May Day comes anyhow, its shorn sheep on the jade slopes and swallows above them following the knell of a leader who knows reasons none ever ask. And the queen cannot cry. Why should the sheep ask, how can they, why the thin man at the end of the lane shears their coats always at just this time of year when it might still be cold and the rains don't stop, and they pause and then they pour and stop and start, and the shaved animals tremble. They never ask why their infants are never satisfied or when they will be killed. And the queen never asks the crazy girl to dance.

~

        The husband of the silenced wife cries like a dove at the far end of the table. Why was she silenced, who tore her tongue out of its brain, why did her blood move in the wrong direction, how will he fill a table for his daughter now, for all the days now, not just on a May Day when the roses are all open, and the communal soup is warm? Why isn't the queen crying? The other diners don't ask their neighbors, don't ask the husband, and they don't ask the queen why she doesn't cry. They wait for a little more southern wine. A little more music, but the strings are breaking.

~

        The queen hoots like a wind between stones. Her guests continue to dine. It's May Day after all. At the end of the long meal, she stands, like a tree in a wind only she feels. She gathers her long robes around herself, she bends down to pick up her mewling animal, she holds it, it stops making any sounds, and the queen wants to say something. She stutters like a faucet turned on after a long winter. She lifts up the most precious thing she has. Her small animal.

        She makes room among the dishes on the long wooden table and she lays it there. It doesn't struggle or fight her, it's an obedient familiar. Cut him into pieces, she tells her people. Please, cut him into pieces, each of you with your own good knife. I want you to know that I give him to all of you for the return of spring. For the tears I can't give. They obey.

~

        They kill the animal. And as night comes next, the aged nightingale, like a clock reset, remembers its role, the one it forgot the night the silent wife first fell to her floor and lost all names and lost all words. It will sing.

It was known, and told, how nightingales will compete with one another for the sweetest songs, all night. And that one who loses the competition often dies. But this night there will be none who try. No rivals. None will compete. It is simply the last night, now. On the highest branch in the kingdom a nightingale remembers its aria and begins. But to all who hear, it has a different voice, a changed sound, sound of a pearl throated dove—not an aria at all. A slow song of mourning.

~

The silent wife who will never speak again is cold but she cannot ask for a cover and she cannot remember her own daughter or her husband or their names, she's a stone, being coated in lichen. A land before the drought. She lies on her cot, no movement at all, and she dreams that she is a cat divided into small pieces for the queen's May feast, and that she is going home with each one of her unquestioning country neighbors. Her husband cries but that changes nothing.

And the queen hisses at the dark that doesn't come anymore. There will be only days now, a time reversed, and a queen, unable still to cry. Her subjects know that her sacrifice was of no use.
The castle doves are obedient. They know their roles. They will cry instead of her. In a kingdom soon known for no nights. Ever. Dry mornings and that sound none want to listen to.
A few things forgotten. Nightingales. Rain. Names.

Did I ever have a name, the daughter asks her father, husband of the silent wife. No one else will tell her. She is about to become a woman. She is about to bleed for the first time. Like the crazy girl she watched, long ago, she almost remembers that day—now alone at the foot of the castle bridge, and bleeding, she has begun to dance.

~

—3—

Paris, Chérie

Kiss-humping bridges,
now you carry this
burned body to a violining dawn rise
in front of Saint Gervais' bells.

Now you monologue to the sex-legged
revenant,
home from her begging.

Home from the dead.
Now you mourn with the massacred
and their white-eyed children.

But courtyards, cathedrals, doorways:
make room, today for the corner-pissing
mendicant.

She needs as much cleanliness
as the shutters—opening.
Kneeling, grate-sleeping,

she needs covers.
You have given me cake, Paris.
Given me mothers.

Given me filthy poems,
barely brave
enough to be written—but I have.

Will you give her a morning-rise
whistle—and promise her one
last lover, one last day, too,

before this year bulges its hips
into next year, and I lose you again,
Paris, darling?

We are both hungry.
Both stained by your autumn hope.

And if you don't —
there are
flames who will.

~

On Evenings of Exceptional Calm

This
is where it lives

cello string still
shuddering flocks
from a high window

where from the lips of silence
stitches—tear,

where there were seahorses rocking
sand into dust, promising rides
no horizons, no falling off —

When now the starfish lie
shadowed on the lowest sands under-sea
no horizons no rising,

no cut-a-limb — and one grows back
not now   but their watered   stilled arms
None know why any more than

water *My generation knows*
we'll be poisoned later or now
the young lean nearer

I'm remembering running
I'm making the effort to remember
a god To breathe through the blank heart

To forgive *Poisoned*
she says And so do I

So we'll go everywhere she says
swim in any sea, she says *dying later or soon*

or not she says When we who
know it's on the way rise
where the starfish bathe

Where the seahorses
male and swell-bellied-pregnant
brood and labor a violent birth

Where the seahorses
dare to let a child
pretend to ride

~

STILLED SUMMER

Every childhood achieves something great and irreplaceable for humanity. —Walter Benjamin

— not martyr martyr martyr martyr martyr — killed-in-the-course-of-attack true-believer, not a *man who loved the homeland, and God loves him, dear, a martyr : regaining presence in the only home left* — not who erases the sun and who holds — who erases the sun and who holds its gun — when the spider is biting her thread? dear —

of children smeared with — walls smeared with — homage — smeared

— not — some call it land of milk, some, of honey, some of greed or where
across another wall, on walls, a bullet's nest, a martyr's
frame, a word some say means witness, written a hundred
times, on a hundred guns,

on children smeared with — walls smeared with — homage — hands —
fat with fat round apples for teachers fat with shells, for the peace of — no peace, ever
now

or what's
— *he carried out a martyrdom operation?*
or what's
the word *mine?* and what's *yours?*
where the spider swallows her thread?

What difference between words and frames and walls?
What's resistant, or martyr, or murder, or God, or
orphan among thorns? Shade in a desert of lame trees

wet as mourning, dry as guns —
where the spider bites — where the summers can
wash under sun's bewildered murders?

It's a museum I tell myself — it's world — once gardens of once
kings, once children.

Gun or grave or war or holy, which of you haunts
harder — home for the weeds?
or the rock's blue blossom?

Which guns not broken to scythes, which war not to
end lies, not still, and no holy land, no, not another — spider —
spitting her thread.

Stilled, in fat-grained sands.
Summer's overgrown good talon.
Heaven-hung effigy, un-
knitted from its bone, bone no
longer sleeved in flesh,
flesh no longer runner
in a tall wheat quiet, in its
night-net web, tinted blue
by a felled moon. The spider
biting her thread.

~

A Place It Might Be All Right To Die

Let a breeze of shoreline locusts
come —

waiting to drown in its blue caved fame,
waiting where the boatman Charon

leans —
Nods *da-da-da-da* —in this water's loose

tongue, hisses yes, the lagoon, yes, where
no dogs howl, yes, yes, inside it, yes

the cerulean, yes, its layers, and yes,
not dreamed. Led in

by an underworld myth —the many
all live in these bays, naked.

Homeless,
would I? Circled, why
did Ulysses ever go home?

Here the fish swim swivel-necked,
follow, under the indigo, follow

for broken-backed sapphires torn
wide by desire — where the sulfur smile lines

shine. And I dive
to tongue unwritten myths,

I dive for their men under chutes
of blue waters. Let the gulls

tell lies
to my impatience.

Let my body mourn
desire.
Let the breeze of shoreline locusts

quicken my tongue —in place of
seductions. In place of blood.

Cave that has no bullet holes
but song—   call me in—.

Isn't this where the ferryman led
between veils and the rock-faced dead?

Boatman of a driven woman's layers,
let the sailors who once kissed

Circe kiss me. Once,
before the summer sun drowns

~

Before Noon

from a tallest branch of the oak
whose leaves will make no wreath
through the lowest black cloud
brush of a barn-owl's wing tip cuts
under the same wide sky
that lists to blood-fall of a beheaded
son— his mother's stone
reach— but that must be another nation
another sound— this wide meadow
only breathes a breeze
only white morning glories open
with moths, their arms, their silent count.

[for James Wright Foley/photo journalist /October 18, 1973 – c. August 19, 2014]

Yes, the Lights

I would fill my mind with thoughts that will not rend.
(O heart, I do not dare go empty-hearted) —Rupert Brooke

Yes, the Christmas lights hang ahead of the hearts.
The boots for war are sweating.

I know.
C'est la guerre. They said so then—They say so, now.

I don't know
What bandages to fold, what wounds to wrap.

I know, *c'est la guerre.* They said so then—they say so
Now. Burned breaths. Dry autumn, beneath.

There is an ancient tradition of filling the cracked bowl with
Gold—to honor what has broken. What is known. We have

Broken again. Blood-moon. Hunter moon. Ecliptic
Hour—like a hummingbird hung over the shoes of war

Standing still. Shared prayer, hear me.
I fear me.

Lights hung ahead of shrouds, *c'est la guerre,* but not
Yet—not now. Don't hear me.

Is Paris back to normal? No, darlings, not at all.
Not anything near normal, not at all. That, we know.

And no bomb of ours or of theirs and no gun will heal it.
Blood moon, hunter moon, filling our cracks with gold.

Will you fill our cracked bowl?
Fill it with a liquid for our vein of burned love.

Paris /November of 2015

Stopped for Hours—

White coals on the tongue.
Gallop of the broken-legged-

Justice-horse
Unbound from flesh.

Yes, bringing dirt.
Yes, singing.

Yes, crows in their cold trees
Stilled only by the breaking

Winter bell. Hissing for respite
Again. Again. Again.

Last week's papers are
Shrouds to wrap old fish.

Lady justice
Splayed.

If you've watched, count the days.
If she stands

Count her shame.
If you've seen the crumbling

Mountain, if you've watched
While she rends her clothes, keening—

Soft pulp, wound in wires of the lies we
Know. While the phoenix-wings
Open — hands — up.

In the stilled hour
When each is too many

We know the voice
Starving— to fight.

The dirt dawn news with its good new scythe.

~

12—2014

[Dec. 29, 2014...Missing Air Asia jet Probably Sank...]

A hundred sorrows under a single sail... —Kuan Hsiu 832-912— *(translation by J.P. Seaton)*

Ten December noons since
another flotilla of coats and dresses
in the same south-east sea,

its retreat that emptied beaches
its strike when the eager
ran for all the sudden fish

its wave that hurried forward
and the hungry water ate —

Page one: another meal
for the gullet of a starved sea
page two another winter

fed to what ravenous minor
Triton? But the drowned float
only to page one now—
syllables stacked for burning—

Night-boats, when
fishes might later be netted,
later, with wedding rings
deep in their bellies

swimmers who might have blessed,
eyes with not a question left
but whispers for
gods who have none

when waves and blind clouds
mouth expected sentences
~ a brave New Year ~
all blessings.

~

After Fado, at the Elgins

He's humming the *saudade*, we're stopped
at horses, and men—my friend who loves

men I who love men and
I am your friend I say, I know, he says, so

few say it, he says I know, I say, the fierce
ballet of muscled legs, genitals capturing each

of our wants—in limestone. How have your
days been I say not your *succès d'estime* or

your failed crowns or mine—I'm weary of
celibacy he says, eyes on the Elgin Centaurs,

battling warrior-boys forever—father, forever,
son, it's war for men he says,

elder—tested to a kill by a perfect boy's fist,
the centaur's heft and metaphor winning—

youth proving, and proving,
but neither older or younger

follow me home now he says I know, I say,
but days, some simple days, a noise of water

running green to its garden pool, pearl
moans of folded wings, an astonishment of early

blossom—don't believe me, I say, reaching no hand
but this kindred-sister-lust toward horse, and man,

whatever age, old friend
                —we adjust our shawls,

turn separate spines on men and centaurs and warriors,
our age and mortal youth, our unto-death un-killed

desires,   old friend, walk me to some square of peace
—there's one around the corner,

                stand before its lack of battle
black tulips, its blooms, its city petals

     —and thank you for your human eye not
other than God's I think, or mine...tell me I say what's lost...

                ~

Beyond My Used-up Words...

Keening with the fallen.
And that is not enough.

Then how will I sleep or write of herons?
Tides, torn in an angry sea's claw. Stilled

flesh whitening
where the wild orchid rises and withers,

her tiny many mouths along a single stalk—
a chorus — all its stilled children

call for any god to reach them.
Breaths stopped — no murmurs left —

and that is not enough.

~

When I see you, my breath tears
there between your bodies.

If I say
what I know of plenty and of empty,
how will I sleep, or dream of herons?

Leaps cut down
curled— used— on the bright,
of road blood stilled in its breeze.

Be
safe this day,
friends, don't curl

and don't be killed
not this day, not after. There will be
cold wakings when your fist will haunt all

sleep. When the dun silence will leave.
I mean to see you
if ever I cannot stand.

This side of the new-born stream
there's no blood yet.

But let our cry
carry.
Infant, in its clairvoyant's caul.

Let our knowing— bleed.
How can we sleep, or write of the fallen?

I am without skin
today.
Your drum— deeper, and going deeper in.

And that is not enough.

There is a place where the wing tears.
And there is a day when the heron stands.
And there is a river for revolution

—the hardest love, coming in.
Bring me to the river where lives begin, where
our nakedness needs no skin, bring me to

where it begins and begins. Nameless. And coming in.
At the end of the beginnings, we dress in long light—
a hybrid body of stars— River, where the parched

heart drinks her fill,
hill where the unborn
climb.

~

— 4 —

Born By Knife

I'm not broken, I lie. I believe the lights meant to love me.
Say I believe I'm a good woman. Empty.
I'm not a selfish child.
My wings were never cut, never burned.

Surgeon, when you opened the redhead's belly to deliver me,
did I look like I belonged? She taught me passages to mourn:
the good, the merciful, the meek, peace making.
When I never knew lava, its pulse, waiting. When I never knew
forsythia. When I never knew any changes as golden, as carriage.

I will learn again as if this mind had rooted with the last apples,
learn newly how to swallow the goodness of green, its boat,
its invented passages, the good, the merciful, the peace-making.
Open me, gods or killers of—does it need knives? Open my eyes
to the island of—tide of—unborn love, where I kneel
to a wide field. Be kind to me. I am returning. The dying
poet amongst us loses her way at birth.

Monet, thick secret of green weeds— a rowboat
with one oar, always ready. Oh, old man, going blind with color:
now, help me paint the water I am treading— help me bare tears
—like teeth, when my ankles are weakening. When love looks extinct.
Can I give up scripting history as though it were old flesh only
Fire-ants nest? Oh, bring me in, like clean wheat.

~

Shears

A feather cape of shade,
each leaf pulled from a dun bird's elegy,

small-stitch sewn by
hands of the hills of Laugharne,

tide-bare shore in
retreat from his heron's prayer.

This is not yesterday's deep burial cave of
stones and kings or gods or voices of Neolithic

hisses, not the wind-scape wash of Pentre Ifan
its hushed rain dolmen,

— this is the poet's perch, his chair, his jacket, his
torn sheets unfit to sing

this is the bed he turns in now— wooden
marker for headboard, a silhouette of

the neighbor daughter's shears trimming
grass under cloud falls that make what light

is there—
explode, call it setting

star, call it his late home.
Remember how he said— *I have a real secret,*

I can fly—
before his heron sanctified his shore.

Now, only someone's daughter
clipping grass with giant shears loud as

wind and dove-moan and silence—
—mine, on a slope beside the poet's cross,

that peace that passeth middle age
and God, so quickly.

We have seen the estuary, haven't we,
where river joins sea, where near,

there's a mound, his breath
interred in the wind.

One cloud-exploded star,
call it sun, while the rook passes

to one repetitious
mourning dove's chant.

A metal voice of
someone's daughter's shears.

~

Half Moon Holy

When the boats drown and their runaways
can't fly When springtime's April fledgling has
crashed on my sill, crying for mother, broken,
when a tree in another grass is axed like the boy
it was planted to remember—shots in his spine,
the leaden whine of not being able to fly—
how to mourn—of all the dyings this time
I worry for the starving fledgling who hasn't
learned a language yet of sky
What if he doesn't know what an enemy
is? I am not your enemy, I told the woman
defending her holy land as the only—
I had shown her the film—Jehovah's
children chanting Death to Palestine, death
to all Arabs— I am not your enemy, I said
but when will you learn how to cry for them
When tonight the temples of Katmandu
drown in the earth, when their climbers
drown under our planet's avalanche,
I am not your enemy, I shout at my sky
and it hisses Which of us must listen
when the breath stops— you or I?

~

My Friends Speak

The island of scientists has named the most detailed map extant —
our place in the universe—
ours— our dripping in human kindness
way, ours, our milky night of innumerable moths—

named it
Laniakea —heaven—immeasurable, heaven, immense —
like Uriel, my friend says, like Daniel.
Descendants of God.

I head for the meadow to not watch the descendants
with knives. To not see the children. Guns in their eyes.
To not see eyes. A million moths,
like circles of hardened stars.
Immeasurable as prayer catchers. Gods.

How large—is it? Speak: stone. Speak: tired bird.
The moths melt like butter across hot meadows, my friend says.
So that we do not watch the chill, spilling from sons,
do not see knives that slice sleep.

Across seas my friend whispers—is love
possible— and someone says well yes, and someone, well no,
and my country has borders, and my country is at war, you see.
Oh speak: stone. Oh speak: tired bird.

In the mean streets of the city of hot light—a graffiti of letters like
locusts shouts *l'amour est mort.*
I will paste the crippled god of peace beneath their wings, will
scrawl instead: *you say "love is dead,"* I will whisper like a stiletto: love
harder in case it is our last chance.

ONE BLESSING

: nightfall to the frozen heron

NATIVE

Skeleton under an older scar. None home but a mouthful of stars. Stars are the bones of the ancestors, we said—under so much night. A geranium pot falls from its sill, dirt, and roots, and pottery, and soil, full petals useless now, all scattered as body parts are after a terrible event. We know too many events. I try to memorize a garden. A volcano never dies, it rests. Rest. You are never too heavy in my arms. How tall the candlenut tree has grown in my absence. Space between its darkling leaves still wanting to be that holy purple. And to remember me. How I wanted to remember how to pray. Come through a ghost's door. Give me to the wind. I have already had—homes. Now, spine to the moon, too bright. River—between hours of dog and wolf, is where I dream of dead healers. And invent God, again. And again. The wars return to their soil to keep on growing. It is the skeleton that holds on longest to its native land.

Almost Untitled/ But Never Without Flames:

What the new holds in her claw
I pretend I never saw before
not the gunned children's empty now
open armed embraces,
not the trace of last year's ash for poets,
fallen holiness, or architects of quiet
shards in buried glass,
not insistent songs with
diminished music but,
again, we are on either shore,
you and I, both,
of the channel again, after eves of
the year the world did not end again,
waving our long feathers and howling
love again   what else can the elder
phoenix once un-grown dinosaur or oily
sand—do? May our flames be lovely.
Now. Always. And again.

~

ADAPTATION

Emergent. Or sorrow or honor how we meet

on boundaries of.

Who, exactly are the great dark birds?

~

—5—

For Sisters Everywhere, Even On St Valentine's Day

You're asleep. Dreaming of being a woman who owns her own womanhood. Dreaming of when you were so young a virgin girl and four friends, all virgins, all made a pact—all inserted their forefingers into their vaginas in a repressive country, under a dictatorial sky, so you could be the ones to take it first. So you would be the ones to own it, still.

And still you dream of it. Still dream of how in hills of that land where you were born, fathers gave their daughters to their neighbor men and those men, their daughters in return so that each man would have a virgin to plummet, a sea to conquer. A skin to open wider than any sky.

And how those girls were lifted onto horses before they would be mounted, were led forward on horses, and each wore the bright red hat of virginity. And each father pulled her forward, pulled her on the horse, to be owned. How in the center of the road, the reins exchanged, the girls belonged, each, to another man. You are asleep. And you are dreaming that you are free.

In Passage / Passage / Passage

                                    and ... but maybe

                                    grace.

But Of The River Too

...your body's animals want to get out —Simone Muench

And the child stepping into firelights
wore the late afternoon.
Wore threads of her father's
old ribbons,
ties to a floating balcony
she waved from.

Her short socks were starved cats,
her breaths
fed by the neighbor's tossed raw liver bits.
Her pinafore was made of walls.
Her lace gloves bought on autumn's boulevard
were made from the thin
white hairs of the lost mothers.

It had been a time of infection
and everyone
was suspected.

We are good people
aren't we?

~

Only Looking For Her Double Headed Tribe,

 . . . Woman of minds,

and so am I—

Blason

If I'd known you when the island
first scraped at my foot soles its sheer

thumbs, hungry fishes — known you
when its thin stones first fell to my hands

under waterfalls and the wide winged
black frigate's flight watched

if I was learning—if I knew you then
knew how to listen   it was as syllables

of a road I hadn't pronounced yet
but I would

fell—it has taken small
houses, roads you lived beyond one

one noon while winter fell in your garden
you sent me on to this one

this rim of a water that knows there are islands
in the long-clouds that know the herds of lost

poets their harsh songs of desire and
how it hurts to not sing them

In the silence of rooms you built with
syllables, and fires, and vixens, and nights,

my steps listen
to winds and the bats guiding light

to your garden's wet growing, even without
eyes—in such a quiet, elder,—celadon roads

that have no names I can learn except a scent
of hawk, a carol of orioles bows— I bow

to one who has parted weeds for me even
at a distance, parted hours, let me walk slowly

hands
open behind you

—for WS Merwin

~

Straw Bird Of Shadow, Be An Owl

Look how it grows, listen to its howl.
There is no
body.

But I am lying.
Today, I killed a lifting before my wheels hit it
winged thing I know I did —

confessed to every horizon and minion
and wouldn't-stop-car-wheels-behind-me,
wheels ahead and a single lane winding down

mountain, broken before me before I could
brake, un-winged.   Murdered in its fall,
a green silence, all sun, there was no

longer a pearl necked up-soar—which nest
listened? Which god? Injured, by one of its own.
When the irradiant ocean black-rain spills—

birds turned to stone—throats, eyes, wings—
weave our cries of continuity—work our braids,
build our nests, wind the willows through our wounds'

memory while someone's heaven hums un-tuned.
While live oaks, one eyed, twist like pythons
belly down wide, silenced, again.

An America, again, an *other*, injured by its own.
A chapel stained incarnadine, open, under
iodine sheets. Open under its walls.

Its rest-in-the emptiness spilled violets, its
poisoned sea anemone eating dark canvas,
shrouds and all. Because we can, we ask when.

Because I am old now, my texts are shawled
Because I can — I will not pretend to die or join
the nests of souls, killer or killed.

Promise me to be happy   I promise I said.
Bothered about beauty. Hungry. Wide, ahead of
elegy. But I lie.   Today.   Ahead of a risen rain.

~

It Was The Door Of Faith, And

—a bird which died advised me to commit flight to memory —Forough Farrokhzad

Leaf-fall-fire, scratching at my skin that will not fall.
Barely blonde, lucent as a hiding stag, its sky crossed by an ink scrape of wings.

~

Here, girl, you said. Here.	I'm old to be the girl, I said.
Sit with the branch, you said.	Heavy with fruit flies.
Heavy with mango water.	Fat mango-flesh-colored gods. All their thumbs,
	twisting.
Rubies of spittle in their beaks.	Hungry nightingales biting their way out of
	a sun-fire's chain.

But there were no nightingales. Only owls.

Hands. Only—their hands.	It was the door of faith.
What was it you wanted?	A field of cellos.
A field of cellos.	It was the door of faith.
A road of biting owls.	An unborn pale cat.
I'm your valley, you said.	And I left you, —I said.

I'm still, still always green. Always wet. Always green.

I wanted —I said.   A night church before anyone dares pray in her again.
But where my mouth longs to open.   But where a landscape bends, untamed.

~

I'm spotted with foreign autumn rust, I said.   Scraping at my skin, I said.
Blood, darling. You said.   Yes, I said. Blood.

My breadfruit trees kneel to you, you said.
Ancestors?
Blood.

Black winds.

~

Wings.   But did you love me?
Wings, you spoke. And —kneel.   I knelt. To your wings.
But winds.   But please, did you love me?

But please. But Please.

~

A Promise

Under stars that speared in—
like hunters' blades skinning kill—

Under your fingers that whispered
you are my wife

and I didn't say *but only in the dark*
—where's the line between?

Let your fingers enter my eyes
as though they could pull out the light,

Tied to the deck of your ground
we stood under knives.

I said *we are stars,*
you said *we are hands,*

you said *wife.* I should have
woven. Didn't. Hands broken.

During a proclamation of great love.
But I am whispering

now: the cripple that once
flew is heading for your island. Without eyes.

Let my fingers enter your eyes.
If I blind you this time,
it will only— I promise — be twilight.

Before My Death

Before my death I will have tried to love again. Before my death I will have tried to love again.

Before my death I will have tried to love again. Before my death I will have tried to love again.

Before my death I will have tried to love again. Before my death I will have tried to love again.

Before my death I will have tried to love again. Before my death I will have tried to love again.

STAGE FRIGHT

My wings were never cut, never burned. My voice is not the hoarse croak of the snake bird, her head just above marsh waters. There are no gods of war. I lie. To be loved by the mirror does not wound. To be loved by the body does not wound. It is only a body. That is one lie. There are others. I am the queen of kindness. Look in my eyes. There is no such thing as a body. No such thing as silence. A wound can't be seen. Can be healed. I promise.

Look how it grows, listen to its song. There is no body. There is no silence. A wound can't be seen, it has no blood. It will not grow. It weighs nothing at all. I am the queen of kindness. Look in my eyes.

After a planet breaks, again and again, those without homes sleep well enough under brittle stars. After a planet breaks, earth is for bodies. Those with homes—give them sheets, shoes. For those without legs—they don't need to run. They will learn the new dances. If I am the child of plenty—look in my heart. If I am a child of my time, I didn't inherit its sword, its broken teeth. I am the queen of kindness. Look in my eyes.

Who are you, I whisper. Because I so need to be kind.

EVIL TWIN OF BLUE

It's said only the dark is visible
still unfolding—
second in a month it is the black moon
dark side of me or new or old dust
The old poet I like best is still alive
feeding one cardinal on his bannister
drinking Wulu Mountain tea on his
eighty-ninth birthday—may the mountain's
height and slope give a needed shade,
protection of a holy parent—
his wife is saying adieus to life amid
the rare fronds   she who all in white
he spied across a woven room and
loved after all the others were whispers —tonight
the thousands, distant suns spy on us
all, how far is far away?

It's getting dark/ little thief of starlight —Randall Jarrell

In Custody of the Eyes

Some blind
blackbird they shot
some tree—cut down,

planted to remember one
boy-man   down
one wing, or two

one song, or two
human with one name
or none, loved, and one of

or one eyed and shot
one tree — cut down
at the knees,

its eyes,
in custody.

~

A branch splattered with
blood buds paused inert as
birds with no wings yet.

(Yesterday, the chair was empty)
(Yesterday, the tomb had a body in it.)

You, also
entered its deep shade
Cocoon   Or tomb

Stained linen and no flies and no flesh, instead.
No breath.

You crawled toward day like the famous
eclipse's worm, trembling belly
to April.

Such faith.
Such faith.
In breaking.

~

Mornings After—

Ask, if I cry, who should translate?
Is there an alchemist in our house
      for nothing left?

No name for us, translator
of my twisted tongue and dawn,
      no milk.

Silence, translate the scholar who walks between
once—Birkenau's chilled chimneys of once-upon-order,
once—Auschwitz' modern vast   *nothing*
      there, nothing left.

Once silence. Ask the dissident. Not her sister death.
I am the woman who asks how
close is a death, how
      near is a god.

Asks   does   order   or its shattered
window—shout? Asks what can
the scholar cry? Is there a scientist
      in our house, for nothing left.

Because tidal waves emptied again
last night, because islands of the land of the rising
sun, spun to corpse pieces, house pieces,
      skin.

Because grandmothers who ran in village
lanes, burning, once before, aged
to what the day gorged, then sent back,
      newly washed.

Ready to burn again sons,
without children, lost,
but their radiant chimneys,
        blistering.

Because on the same earth I hold the crow-
born dawn, hold swift-songed morning's fresh
milk, ask, if I cry, who can
        translate? Are there

alchemists in our house? I am
the woman who asks, after.
Sparrow, eye on a god with no name
        for us, what did you find?

Raising Her Eyelids

Without eyes. Who are you, she whispers. Waiters at the local cafe know her and shake her hand. Am the woman who cannot remember a face in his coffin. She tries. She loves small animals, tall blonde grass. And the largest rocks. I am the woman who cannot remember his face in his coffin, there is no face. I am the woman who wears black clothing and picks cat hairs from her sleeves. Who are you. I am the woman, stone in the winter, stone in the summer, a flower in her bed. She lights blood colored candles. The woman who wears her best dress, early in the morning, no one watching. Am the woman who is beginning to— I am the woman who asks, how close is death, how near is God. There is an answer.

When she raises her eyelids, it's as if she were taking off all her clothes. —Colette

One — Will Not Fall

Too chill to be alive the road

said the only mantra it knew

and a bird that would never have

been born sang

Dusk

This is the place. No chairs.
A woman who is choosing
has sent a petal from her bloom
of conscious closing.

The woman who is choosing when
—scratches vellum. The rook stands.
The woman in the nest of
the phoenix hovers nearer
her edge like that brood of birthing

opal-throated pigeons in an empty
flower trough,
thirsty, one stair above my sill,
breaking their shells one by

one. She repeats
my words
from dusk in a jungle where
medicine leaned small against thorn trees.
Each poison growing in a forest

lives beside its antidote, we said.
I am still eager, I said.
Or the scent of hyacinth.
The woman remembering, who is

choosing when to die will
curl before leaves have blood-burned September.
Surrender by starvation,
she doesn't name her illness

only how many days.
Three more. The woman
in worn white cotton washed us in a tide pool,
brewed petals, shouted under

regrets at the edge of rain. Bon voyage to me & love
life as you live it she scribbles blue before her breath
ends a night and a day and the broken slant
dawn.

The woman who was choosing when to die.
Too young to be skeletal, skin taken wing.
Bone no longer needed. Dove.
Fire-eyed. Distant. Opal.

The root does not care
where her water comes from.
Here is another thirsty body.
Broken into morning.

~

Notes:

Soleil cou coupé , by Apollinaire, epigraph for the poem "Cut," might be translated as *Sun, with its neck cut.*

It is the skeleton that holds on longest to its native land, last line in the poem, "Native," is by Rosemarie Waldrop.

Birkenau refers to the Nazi German extermination camp Auschwitz II.

When at night I go to sleep/ fourteen angels watch do keep, is from the Evening Prayer in Engelbert Humperdinck's opera, "Hansel and Gretel."

"Dusk" : A small addendum regarding this poem...A woman I once knew many years before suddenly wrote to me to say that she had come across a poem of mine that had been meaningful to her, and that by the time I received her card, she would no longer be in the body. I began the poem, not knowing if it could be reply or elegy. One week later, I learned that it was to be the latter.

~

Acknowledgments

My thanks to editors of these publications where poems from this book have appeared in earlier versions: *Plume* ("Pulse" & "Whose Sky, Between"), *Prairie Schooner* ("Blason Pour le Corps"), *Academy of American Poets Poem-For-a-Day* [selected by the chancellors] ("Dusk"), *Poets Quest For God Anthology* (Eyewear Publishing) ("Dusk"), *New Letters* ("12—2014," "Paris Chérie," "Yes, the Lights"), *Spillway* ("Mornings After"), *Gulf Coast* ("It Was The Door of Faith, And"), *Tupelo Quarterly* ("Stilled Summer"), *About Place Journal* ("In Custody of the Eyes"), *Still Life With Poem Anthology* ("A Place it Might be Alright to Die"), *Still Against War IV —Poems for Marie Ponsot* ("My Friends Speak"), *Wordpeace* ("Stopped for Hours"), *Aeolian Harp Anthology #1* (Glass Lyre Press) ("Whisper," "Pulse," "Dusk"), *Phantom Limb* ("Almost Untitled"), *Southern Humanities Review* ("No Modifier At All").

About the Author

MARGO BERDESHEVSKY, born in New York city, often writes in Paris. *Before The Drought* (in an early version) was finalist for the National Poetry Series, 2015. Berdeshevsky is author as well of the poetry collections *Between Soul & Stone*, and *But a Passage in Wilderness* (Sheep Meadow Press). Her book of illustrated stories, *Beautiful Soon Enough*, received the first Ronald Sukenick Innovative Fiction Award for Fiction Collective Two (University of Alabama Press). Other honors include the Robert H. Winner Award from the Poetry Society of America, a portfolio of her poems in the *Aeolian Harp Anthology #1* (Glass Lyre Press), the *& Now Anthology of the Best of Innovative Writing*, and numerous Pushcart prize nominations. Her works appear in the American journals *Poetry International, New Letters, Kenyon Review, Plume, The Collagist, Tupelo Quarterly, Gulf Coast, Southern Humanities Review, Pleiades, Prairie Schooner*, among many others. In Europe her works have been seen in *The Poetry Review* (UK), *The Wolf, Europe, Siècle 21, & Confluences Poétiques*. A multi genre novel, *Vagrant*, and a hybrid of poems, *Square Black Key*, wait at the gate. She may be found reading from her books in London, Paris, New York City, or somewhere new in the world. Her "Letters from Paris" may be found in Poetry International, here: http://pionline.wordpress.com/category/letters-from-paris/

For more information, kindly see: http://margoberdeshevsky.blogspot.com/

Glass Lyre Press

exceptional works to replenish the spirit

Glass Lyre Press is an independent literary publisher interested in technically accomplished, stylistically distinct, and original work. Glass Lyre seeks diverse writers that possess a dynamic aesthetic and an ability to emotionally and intellectually engage a wide audience of readers.

Glass Lyre's vision is to connect the world through language and art. We hope to expand the scope of poetry and short fiction for the general reader through exceptionally well-written books, which evoke emotion, provide insight, and resonate with the human spirit.

Poetry Collections
Poetry Chapbooks
Select Short & Flash Fiction
Anthologies

www.GlassLyrePress.com

www.ingramcontent.com/pod-product-compliance
Lightning Source LLC
Chambersburg PA
CBHW051247110526
44588CB00025B/2909